MOTHER MAY I

TINA PARKER

SIBLING RIVALRY PRESS
LITTLE ROCK, ARKANSAS
DISTURB / ENRAPTURE

Mother May I
Copyright © 2016 by Tina Parker

Cover photo courtesy of the author
Author photo by Jeanne Nakazawa
Cover design by Seth Pennington

Sibling Rivalry Press, LLC
PO Box 26147
Little Rock, AR 72221

info@siblingrivalrypress.com

www.siblingrivalrypress.com

ISBN: 978-1-943977-07-9

Library of Congress Control No: 2015960258

This title is housed permanently in the Rare Books and Special
Collections Vault of the Library of Congress.

First Sibling Rivalry Press Edition, March 2016

With love and thanks always to Jason, Iris, and Opal.

MOTHER

MAY I

Stop

No we're not playing baby any more
Get up
You can walk
Use big girl words

Sit down or you're not getting dessert
You have a napkin right there
Why are you wiping your mouth with your sleeve

Why are you doing that
Please let me eat
I need my arm
You're hanging on it

Stop kicking her
You're not going to bite your sister
We don't hit

I don't know why I plan things for you to do
With your friends when you act like this
If you want to hear the song stop talking
Leave her alone

Just close your mouth and be quiet
I'll tell you when to come out
I'm not ready to see you

We're going to turn that off in a minute
You have five more minutes
No there are no more minutes it's time to go
Come on I'm leaving

Just a minute
Get your hands off me
I don't like the hitting hands
Use your words

No I can't
You know how to put them on yourself
It makes my back hurt
Because I'm mean

MOTHER MAY I

Mother may I sit and stare
Out the window
May I breathe
Just breathe
Mother may I read
This poem
Again and again
May I write some lines
Mother will you care for my children
Will you fold our clothes and sweep our floors
Mother may I keep needing you as they need me
Mother if you will only let me
Mother may I
Promise I will not ask
Anything of you again

QUESTIONNAIRE

How many times have you been pregnant?_____

How many children born alive?_____

Stillbirths?_____

Miscarriages?_____

C-sections?_____

Complications of pregnancy?_____

WHEN MY FOUR-YEAR-OLD ASKS
MAMA WILL ME AND OPAL DIE ONE DAY
I WANT TO SAY NO

no you won't but instead I don't say anything
do we need to get old for that she is persistent this is what she wants
me to say but I can't say that because it could be today
salmonella from a cantaloupe or E.coli from a hamburger
my two-year-old pushes beads along colored wire her lips pursed
she picks one color at a time pushes up and down to line them up
she hears us but she is too small to ask questions

What was your childhood lacking the prompt of the day asks
paint sky words a stage on which to dance but how can I give them all
of that something would have to go maybe if I don't exercise

What is wrong
eHow says this is good to ask before the first counseling session
I made them stand still to get their hair fixed
I let their hair go unbrushed
I wake in the night and feel sad
in the day I am restless and drained
I call to check for messages but there are no new
messages at this time

Describe your feelings about the problem
I feel _____   _____
and _____

List the reasons you are seeking help
when I read the older one asks mama why does your face look mad
and when daddy tells her I am a writer she says mama writes store lists
I see the younger one's head slam down the concrete steps
her body mashed by a truck's tires

I see her facedown in the tub
I read a news article about a pastor
who beat his teenage daughter with a shoe
during an argument about her going to a party
and I get it I side with him he pinned her arms and held her down
and then the shoe he just needed her to do what he said

Mama why is the sun so hot my four-year-old asks
it's a ball of fire it's actually a star the sun is not up yet it is still dark
already the bus is pulling children up the hill to our house
first we see the light blink open the trees then the sound of exhaust
like a breath held long and let out we walk toward it and wait
when the door opens she will need to climb the steps by herself
at bedtime I will be ready to sing hush little baby when she stops me
to say mama today on the playground no one wanted to play with me
the sun was in my eyes mama I wish you were always with me

I Am Needed

My shoulders are tight
From pulling away

HER FIRST YEAR

In the early months,
it is suckle and sleep,
suckle and sleep.
We tickle her feet
to keep her awake,
to be sure she has enough.

At the half-year mark,
it is suckle and play.
She bobs on,
and off.
So newly aware
of her world
she must nurse
in the dark,
on an island only
we can rock to.

Thank God her teeth
come late.
I hold her tight
to fight the pain
when she hooks
them in, my blood
on her lips.

At one year,
a final binge
like she knows
it will end.
She'll be okay,
my husband pats her back.

But it's me
I worry about.
It's my breasts,
how they lump
and leak
and throb.
And see how
she plays
and laughs
and asks
for her cup
when I need her
to remember
my body
in hers. Please,

tell me
she will remember
the days,
the hours,
the minutes
I was enough.

WHEN MY FOUR-YEAR-OLD ASKS MAMA
WHY DO YOU HAVE HAIR ON YOUR VAGINA
I DO NOT ANSWER

the first hair will curl
from your armpit
a question mark
no one will answer
next the coarse curls
down there
just enough to detangle
with your finger
it will feel good
to touch them
so good
you stroke pull stroke
without thinking
when a friend
spends the night
she will cry out
what are you doing
this will alarm you
you'll go back
to picking at your hangnails
all through junior high
into high school
finally in college
you will reclaim
that mound
more hair and softer
you will stroke
a better spot
a slick home
just right for one finger

I Wait for Iris to Talk Herself to Sleep

Mama, why is my dreams so hard to see?

Because they're little?

Is my dreams in my pillow?

19

THE STAY-AT-HOME MOM PONDERS
WORK OUTSIDE THE HOME

This mother role.
I think I have to do it all
            the time.
I think I have to give it
            100
per
        cent.

                    Because it was difficult to have them
                    well to conceive her
                    the tests
                    the medicine
                    the shots
                    the K-Y Jelly coated sticks
                    probed   into my vagina
                                 to count
                    eggs   to count
                    sacs   to find
                    a heartbeat to determine
                    gender.

I'm tired
of planning enriching
kid activities.

I no longer enjoy
storytime
or play dates.

I'm tired
of laundry
and store lists.

I'm afraid
I will scar them
          for life

if they are not
with me all
          the time.

(Mama where is the baby before it's in your belly)

PITTING CHERRIES

I dig my thumb into firm flesh,
release the pit. The skin sucks
a sigh of relief. The juice, red
on my fingers, splatters
the cutting board in patterns
like my blood in perfect
polka dots on the floor. It came in a gush
at lunchtime, a crimson line laced
the toilet. My floral skirt
transformed to a thick velvet
curtain over the show.
Somehow the baby's heart beats on,
though my own hangs silent,
a stony vessel ripe for the picking.

First Fight

It was nap time
You told me poo poo
and ran

I caught you
              I held your arms
You twisted
until you went red

Your eyes bulged
              you went boneless

I needed rest
But you would not   stop

I closed the door
To keep you in there

You banged
and shouted   Mama
              Mama come in here

I swung the door in
fast
and caught your toe

I offered to kiss your boo-boo
I tried to rock you
              No way Mama   go away
              Mama

24

You shooed me
with your hand
You'd not take

my lap
or your bed

you slept   belly down   bare legs

on the cold
wood floor

THE DAY MY FOUR-YEAR-OLD SCRATCHED ME

I scratched her back
It broke the skin
I knew I'd be turned in

I prayed it would heal
By the time she went to school

In the tub that night she cried
Oh my boo-boo hurts
How did I get this boo-boo mama

She said maybe from my hair thing
When it was on my wrist

And I did not correct her.

My four-year-old and her friend
compare their birthmarks

in the bathroom, pants around their ankles.
Look Teddy, I have one too, my little girl points
to the purple blue thumbprint on her bottom.
Yours is bigger, she says of the blush red
cloud over both his cheeks.

It's big, but it will get smaller, he shrugs
and waits for me to pull up his pants and snap
the metal button on his jeans.

(Mama will you die first because you're older than daddy)

The Monday after Newtown

OUR DAUGHTER GETS READY FOR SCHOOL

"Is there ever a right day,
I mean you just do it, you know,
get them back to school."

- Peter Muckell, Newtown parent

She goes into her room
Comes out holding a blanket under her chin
Mama look I wanted to surprise you
She drops the blanket and shouts
Purple all purple Mama
She puts her hands to her chest to prompt me

Purple shirt?   Hands to her knees
Purple pants?   To her feet
Purple socks?

We agree to do it
We are the parents
The school sent a letter
Re-establishing routines is a critical part
of getting back to normal

Make beds
Start the wash
Fold clothes
She's not here
She is at school
The phone does not ring

Last night I dreamed   the hallway
The principal and counselor   running
     after him

stop   stop   they would stop him
We conduct regular drills including those for building lockdown
We have secure doors at each entrance
Other exterior doors remain locked at all times

              I was a teacher once
              She had long curly hair
              A boyfriend who broke up with her
              A baby inside her

And here it is
Just say it
Twenty children died
Little children
Near the same age
As our own
And at night when ours go to bed
We do the very thing that can make another

                   When he wanted to meet at the park
                   She brought the ultrasound picture
                   And he shot her in the head
                   Shot her dead across from the school

Our students and your children are our most precious resource
Certainly in this day and age we can never
Be absolutely protected against all circumstances

The phone does not ring
She is at school
I hear her voice in every room
Bye Mama Bye Opal
I'll see you when I get off the bus
Bye-bye
I'll give you a hug and a kiss
when I get home.

QUESTIONNAIRE

How many times have you been pregnant? _____3_____

How many children born alive? _____2_____

Stillbirths? _____0_____

Miscarriages? _____1_____

C-sections? _____0_____

Complications of pregnancy?____Subchorionic hematoma____

31

Ten Centimeters: His Story

How she begged, get someone to check me
I didn't want to get the nurse
I didn't want to get her hopes up
I rubbed her back
I helped her to the toilet
Many times to the toilet
I helped her climb onto the bed
On all fours her butt in the air
I would've helped her climb the wall
But there were cords

The nurse came in looked at her ass
In the air and knew she was close
We've got to get the midwife
She called for Nancy
It sounds funny but she did
She called for the midwife and said
Wait   wait
Don't let her start pushing
By then she was so crazy
I knew she would never hear
But I got close to her ear   she's here
Nancy's here
And that's something I did
That's something I gave her

Unspoken

The women sit side-by-side
on the porch. One small, folded
into herself, her white hair in wisps
about her head. She reaches
a hand out, her fingers crooked
at the joints, her movement in slow
time. Her face keeps its firm lines,
but her eyes flicker when her hand
rests on the younger one's belly.
She feels life rolling there and recalls

the ones she has lost.
She does not speak the names
to her granddaughter. How can she know
their lives have been so much the same?
They have both known the quickening
of the womb too soon, the blood that washes
out but does not cleanse.

You'll enjoy this baby so much more being older.
She'll be nothing but a blessing to you.
Her words tumble into the quiet space
and her hands fold back into her lap.
Both women sigh, their rockers creak
as they raise their heads to the darkening sky.

GIFT

Mama I made you a red heart wrapped
in a purple sky.

JUST FOR PRETEND

She wants me
In her lap.

She wants me
To be her baby.

She sits back
Into the couch

Gets a pillow and I lay my head
In her lap.

She says baby sad
And waa-waa I wail my baby cry

To get her wet lips to kiss
My cheek.

She drools
Into my mouth

And that's when I know
I am in love with her.

She has not yet lived
Three years but already

She knows how to make me stop
And let myself be held.

(Mama why am I born)

MY FERTILITY DOCTOR, SHE IS A GENTLE GOD

who gives out babies
except one day
she has a resident-in-training

    will it be okay
    if he examines you

and too quick the K-Y Jelly coated stick
is in and he whips it around like he's digging
a hole

    don't forget there's a person
    on the other side of that

don't
forget

he slows and the screen lights up
she counts eggs
she writes how many
and on which side
he yanks the stick out
before I can say

stop
I want a baby
the normal way

How To Get Two Toddlers in the Car

Hold one by the arm
(she will refuse your hand)
Hook your foot around the other's ankle
Open the car door

Offer a sucker for the first one seated
Let go of the older one so she can climb in
Unhook foot and take the younger one's arm
Give her bottom a push as she climbs in

        Mama I want a purple sucker
Just a minute

Tell the younger one to get right in her seat
Open the back hatch to retrieve her
Remind her about the suckers
Tell the older one to put her arms into arm straps

        Mama I want a purple sucker
Just   a   minute

Take the younger one by the arm
Give her bottom a push as she climbs in
Buckle her seat belt
Close the door and walk to the other side of the car
Open the door

        Mama I want a purple sucker
Just a _____   minute

Buckle the older one's seat belt
Close the door
Walk to the driver's door

38

Open the door
Get in
Check your bag for suckers

We'll get some at home
                Can't we get some at the bank
No it's closed

Drive home
Stay there

DROP MY NAP

I stay up late
I wake in the night
And play in my bed
It could be time
To drop my nap
If I appear irritable
Or cranky please
Put the nap back in

WHILE MUCH OF THE WORLD GOES TO WORK

I take my three-year-old to the park
She chases ducks
How they squawk and run
She laughs when they sink their beaks
Into their backs
She sits with them
Under a big oak
A breeze lifts off the water
And the sun makes the lake dance

She lets a worm crawl on her shoe
And up her leg
She wraps its body in knots
She wants to take it home
The worm lives here, I say
Let's find a safe place for it
She hangs it from a pine branch
Bye-bye worm
She grabs my hand
And leads me laughing
To the car

Mama I'm so sad I don't want to
think anymore

I don't want to think of not having my mommy
And my daddy and Opal
I want to be a mermaid and live forever
I wouldn't be able to swim with my Paw and Ganny
Or play with Opal or go on the stage
How could I go away and not do those fun things anymore
I wouldn't be able to think anymore
How could I still remember it

Hour of Need

Life pulled at my shirt
Lifted it and sucked
From my breast
We rocked through death

Uncle JD was first
His lungs filled
He drowned in that water
The trip too far
We rocked despite his death

Then Uncle Jack
He got cancer all over
Aunt Sue scattered his ashes
On the New River
We rocked
Their lips hungry at my breast

Aunt Poochie passed
In her house dress and slippers
I don't know what took her
My daughters drank and grew strong
O how they ran and laughed

My best friend's father next
Like an uncle
He drove us to the mall
And called his women heifer
We rocked through his death

I hoarded life
I held it to my chest
I never grieved them
So I carry them still

They are my dead
Their weight pulls
Curdled milk
From my breasts

You've Pulled Away from Me Again

Your hand all your own now.
I see a flash of mint green,
your back in a coat I have zipped
again and again.

I hear your feet on the pavement.
Your laughter begs me to chase you.
You have run to the other side
of the car where there are other cars
and I do not know if you will stop.

WHEN OUR FIVE-YEAR-OLD ASKS
IF THERE IS MORE SKY OR GRASS

We pause before answering
Share a look
O what a poetic
Child we made

    More sky it goes on forever
    Into infinity
    But more water than anything

She does not answer
Only asks
Can we have cookies for dessert?

JUST LIKE THAT I HAVE A DAYCARE BABY

Only she's not a baby
She's four but still
Some other woman gets her
Breakfast and lunch and snack
And fixes her hair when the clip falls out
I don't know what she plays all day
Or what she says or whether the other woman
Talks nice to her for all I know she yells at her
She could be sad
Likely she misses me
But Mama works in an office now
It is quiet here
I have time to pour coffee
And put creamer in
I have time to drink it
Sometimes I even make it
I get paid to do this
I wash coffee mugs
The brown stains are stubborn
But there are no interruptions
I can close the door to my office
If I need to concentrate
Say I need to read or write
I put up a sign:
      I need to concentrate
      But if you need me
      Please come in
No one comes in.

JOY

after Naomi Shihab Nye's "Kindness"

Before you know what joy really is,
you must have much loss.
You must feel the future a wide pool
waiting to take you under.
How you kick and flail
toward your dreams while
the smiling people lounge and wave,
just out of reach.

Before you learn the unforeseen comfort of joy,
you must travel to your core
where a baby lies curled, unsleeping
yet unawake. You must see how this baby
is a part of you, how her blue skin echoes
the flecks in your eyes, feel with certainty
that you, too, will die.

Before you know joy as the deepest thing inside,
you must know loss as the deepest thing.
You must hold loss, a furred heap in your lap.
You must call its name out the back door
until your voice grows hoarse and you catch
just a glimpse of its tail wagging in the distance.

Then it is only joy that makes sense anymore,
only joy that takes your hand, leads you
to the kitchen window to show you a red-
gold sunrise. Only joy that nods its head
in the back of the room to say I am here
to cradle you, to grow you strong.
I am here to hold you closer than the womb.

ON THE MORNING OF OUR YOUNGEST DAUGHTER'S THIRD BIRTHDAY

Scrub the toilet
Make beds
Wrap presents
Dress the girls
Fix their hair
Make French toast
Finally the kitchen clears out
It is me and her
She wants to play baby
I lift her onto my lap
My hand presses her head to my chest
I bend at the waist to rock us back
And forth in the ungiving kitchen chair

          I carried her in my body
          I held her first
          I birthed her and I nursed her
          She is mine

She pulls her head off my chest
To look into my eyes
Mama what is that
Why is your face dripping

          There will be no more
No more babies from this body

Shhhh it's okay baby
She lets me hold her
And I rock us
Into the gray light
Of another December morning.

DECISION

The girl in the chair is six, or seven
Her red hair pulled back from her face
To feature her ears
Her mom is there
>   You're going to be so excited.
>   Here, squeeze my hand.

There are purple dots on her ears
Do those look even with her face
The woman asks. She pulls on her gloves
And the girl begins to cry.
>   Squeeze your bear.
>   Squeeze my hand.

My girl is five
She has not moved only watched
She will not speak for some time
But when she does her decision releases me
>   Mama I want to be older than you
>   When I get my ears pierced.

$$\left(\text{Mama when will I grow up} \right)$$

I AM JUST BEGINNING TO SWEAR OFF RESTAURANTS WITH INDOOR PLAYGROUNDS

when a woman turns in her booth
she says
we lost a son
he battled cancer twelve years
they just kept finding it
but you do the best you can
day by day
you enjoy them.

When Iris wheezes she will not do
her inhaler

she runs and I say
we have to do it

we'll do it the hard way   I hold her down
I put the mask   to her face

she can breathe now
                    and more   she screams

I want to do it
let me do it
I'll do it the easy way
please mama
                    please

how she stomps
and wails
she can't stop

she won't let me
hold her
no she says no
she doesn't need
a nap
she doesn't want
to sleep

I lift her in my arms
all
            four feet
of her

look a squirrel   I see
a squirrel
on the tree

I sway
our bodies
together
her feet
              to my knees

she puts her head
on my shoulder

mama let's sit down
together

I MEANT TO TELL YOU

I saw a blue heron
On a rock in the creek
Its wings went wide
To fly from me

I meant to tell you
I saw a deer
A white flicker
In the brush

I meant to tell you
But you were in the shower
And then you were at work
The girls needed their nails clipped
And now you are asleep.

AT BREAKFAST WE TALK ABOUT OUR DREAMS

I dreamed there were a bunch of potties out in the yard
All our friends were out there
And they each had their own potty

    I dreamed I was running late my friend was about to perform
    But I needed a shower the bathroom was locked
    And I didn't have my shampoo or toothbrush

I dreamed my hair was all white
Like Gigi's and I saw a video of my life
I saw me and Opal
And when Teddy came to our house to play

    I dreamed Daddy was going to have a baby
    But he was hardly showing and I was so worried
    No one would believe me

I dreamed me and Opal were in the tub
And the water got really high
And the Cat in the Hat came in and we said where's Mama
When's she coming back and he said Never

    I dreamed a highway and me behind the wheel
    The car out of control and me nearly hitting other cars
    Over and over barely missing them

I dreamed you were going away from me
What was that place you were going
You were going away from me
And I could not reach you Mama

Mama seeks counseling to sort her conflicted emotions

No matter what you'll always
Be their Mama
Even if you're not the one to give them that first cup
Of Kool-Aid when they get off the bus
You are the Mama
And nothing can change that

SINCE YOU ASKED HOW I'M DOING NOW THAT
MY DAUGHTER STARTED KINDERGARTEN

I miss her at my side every minute
Mama Mama every minute
In my ear
Will you read to me
Mama when will you play with me
Mama where are you

Those years of work
Now a six year gap
No resume could capture
What I did with that time

See how she gets up early
Excited and ready to go
See how she sings and plays school
After she gets home

Since you asked
I'm not the cursing kind
But I'm fucking sad

Questionnaire

I have two daughters. My first pregnancy ended in a miscarriage after my first cycle of in vitro fertilization (IVF). Iris is my oldest daughter, born after the second cycle of IVF. Opal is my youngest daughter. She was conceived naturally. I refused the birth control pill my OB pushed after Iris' birth: as happy as it would be, would you want to be pregnant when you have a six month old? Opal was conceived when Iris was 15 months old.

Raising Jesus

did you pin his arms
and hold him down
Mary did you smack
his legs did he ever
make you cry Mary
did you take a deep breath
count to ten Mary
I bet you just held
it in didn't you Mary
did you hear him say mama
again and cringe and sigh
were you relieved when
it was a temple day Mary
did you dream those dreams
Mary where you see him
hurt or worse
did you wake in prayer
Mary did you ask God
to let you die first

THE BOTTOM OF THE HILL

My three-year-old waits
Arms open
Come on
Run Mama
I'll catch you.

IN THE MORNINGS I TAKE HER TO DAYCARE
AND WHEN WE SAY GOODBYE SHE KISSES
MY CHEEK BUT TODAY I FEEL HER
EYES ON ME EVEN AFTER I'VE
TURNED TO LEAVE

I look back
Thank god
She's not crying
I smile big
And blow her a kiss
She puts her palm to her mouth
Kisses her hand
She is still holding it there
When I turn away
Her lips clamped around the kiss

MOTHER MAY I
a found poem from Wiki

To begin the mother stands
at one end of the room and turns away
while the children line up at the other end.
The children take turns asking,

"Mother may I _____?"
The mother replies, "Yes,
you may" or "No, you may not,
but you may _____ instead." The children

usually move closer to the mother
but are sometimes led farther away.
Even if the mother makes an unfavorable suggestion,
the child must still perform it.

The first of the children to reach the location
of the mother wins the game.
That child then becomes the mother herself,
the original mother becomes a child,
and a new round begins.

My four-year-old asks what happens when people die and when I hesitate she answers her own question

First they wake up on the day they're going to die
And they pack up all their clothes
And they say goodbye to their mama and goodbye
To their daddy
They go to a different state and find a nice empty
House that's quiet and a good soft bed
And they lay down.

MOTHER MAY I

Acknowledgments

Thank you to the editors of the publications where the following poems first appeared:

PMS: poemmemoirstory ("Raising Jesus"), *Rattle* ("My four-year-old asks what happens when people die and when I hesitate she answers her own question"), *Literary Mama* ("When my four-year-old asks mama will me and Opal die one day"), *Shot Glass Journal* ("I meant to tell you"), *Appalachian Heritage* ("Unspoken"), *The Collapsar* ("Stop," "Her First Year," "My fertility doctor, she is a gentle god," and "I am just beginning to swear off restaurants with indoor playgrounds"), *Circe's Lament: Anthology of Wild Women Poetry* ("Stop" and "The day my four-year-old scratched me"), *MOTIF: All The Livelong Day: an anthology of writings about work* ("Pitting Cherries"), and *Motherhood May Cause Drowsiness: Mom Stories from the Trenches*, Second Edition ("First Fight").

GRATITUDE

To Bryan Borland and Seth Pennington for the phone call I always dreamed of and a journey filled with support and encouragement.

To the Kentucky Foundation for Women for grant support that made this book possible; to the Berea Arts Council for giving voice and space to artists in my community.

To my poetry mentors who give me light and courage: Danny Marion, the late James Baker Hall, Gurney Norman, Leatha Kendrick, Katerina Stoykova-Klemer, and Young Smith.

To my friends for extra eyes and good listening ears: the late Pam Sexton, Sherry Chandler, Shelda Hale, Ann Lederer, Joanie DiMartino, Jean Welch, Nancy Cassell, Steve Rhodes, Leslie Shane, Georgia Stamper, Libby Jones, Barbara Wade, Vicky Hayes, Dorothy Schnare, Leslie Ferguson, Laurel Carlsen, Betsy Coblentz, Dalphna Donnelly, Jeanne Nakazawa, Rachel Dorroh-Sheehan, Becky Gatewood, and Rachael White.

To my family for inspiring me: Jason, Iris, and Opal Bailey. This book was born from love of you.

About the Poet

Tina Parker grew up in Bristol, Virginia, and now lives in Berea, Kentucky, with her husband and two young daughters. Her chapbook *Another Offering* is available from Finishing Line Press. Individual poems have been published in such journals as *Rattle*, *The Collapsar*, *PMS: poemmemoirstory*, and *Appalachian Heritage*. Her poetry has received support from the Kentucky Foundation for Women. (www.tina-parker.com)

ABOUT THE PRESS

Sibling Rivalry Press is an independent press based in Little Rock, Arkansas. Its mission is to publish work that disturbs and enraptures. This book was published in part due to the support of the Sibling Rivalry Press Foundation, a non-profit private foundation dedicated to assisting small presses and small press authors. (www.siblingrivalrypress.com)

CPSIA information can be obtained
at www.ICGtesting.com
Printed in the USA
LVHW040246231121
704213LV00009B/951